To Live on this Earth

To Live on this Earth

Ken Waldman

WEST END PRESS

Acknowledgments

Some of the poems in this collection have been published previously in the following: *Anemone, Appalachia, Barnabe Mountain Review, Chariton Review, Chiron Review, Christ in a Wheelchair, Crucible, ELF, Exquisite Corpse, Fiddler Magazine, High Plains Literary Review, Ice-Floe, International Poetry Review, Louisville Review, Manoa, Old-Time Herald, Permafrost, Poet Lore, Poetry International, Pudding, Quarterly West, Raven Chronicles, Sidewalks, South Dakota Review, Sou'wester, Storyboard, Sycamore Review, Wordwrights, Yalobusha Review,* and *Zone 3.*

Second printing, April 2003
ISBN: 0-9705344-6-9

Book and cover design by Nancy Woodard
Distributed by University of New Mexico Press

West End Press • P.O. Box 27334 • Albuquerque, New Mexico 87125

Contents

The Road, Circa 1978
—*for Howard Nelson*

We'd studied Kerouac, Ginsberg, Kesey,
Hunter S. Thompson, followed Lou Reed,
Frank Zappa, Sleepy LaBeef, the Dead,
known we somehow needed the marathon
drive across West Texas, New Mexico,
Arizona desert, two recent East Coast
college grads guzzling bad coffee
and beer at all hours in forlorn bars,
gambling time that didn't matter
on a geography and spirit that might.
Hitting California midway between
midnight and dawn, an extra-bright
February full moon shone like the ghost
of a lamp as we parked our Dodge van,
slapped hands, and jumped out radiating
caffeine at that cool and shadowy border.
Climbing back in, popping open brews,
we shoved John Coltrane into the deck,
lit another joint, spun the wheel,
then rattled back on the road, aiming
for Los Angeles, the Pacific, beyond.

I

After Hearing John Haines Read

Poet to whom all others are measured
who write of Alaska, he appears tough
as his work, an elemental line, gruff
and lean, an honest being indentured
to land. His speaking voice, long-weathered
by six-month subsistence winters, is rough
and smooth at once, as if wide enough
to embrace both poles. Think rock pressured
by ice and light. Think immensities
mated with silence. Think centuries
of fox, bear, marten, beaver, owl. Picture him
silver as snow gathering on birch limb,
gold as some wolves. Or building a fire
in forty below night. Someplace farther.

Old-Time Fiddle Lesson

To learn, lock yourself
and your fiddle in a room
all winter, and practice
until you play with a twisty
heartfelt rhythmic punch
that approaches trance:
fiddling is not technical
repetition anyone can master—
it's the sound you make
once you know in the blood
you clog with your fingers
while that old devil music
dances inside the box.

Washing Dishes on My 33rd Birthday

Four years now in my Alaska cabin
without running water, I do dishes
lifting a five gallon jug chest-high,
tilting the spigot so water dumps
in the big pot on top the oven.
After lowering the jug, I light
a back burner, play fiddle, await
steam: the start of my Sunday night

ritual. Today I'm 33.
No sink, I slowly raise the pot
of hot water, empty half
in a large bowl I've squirted
with soap, set pot beside bowl
so they rest on front burners

close as man and wife.
Then I soak glasses in suds,
sponge rims, sides, bottoms, dip
insides in scalding pot water,
set on the rack to dry. Next,
plastic yogurt containers, plates,
soup bowls, bread pans, small pots,
bigger bowls, chopsticks, silverware—

a system I stick to. I'm obsessed
with order. When visiting, I'll wash
dishes my way—first glass, plastic, clay;
then steel, iron, wood, silver—pleased
to inflict my weekly routine on hosts,
especially those with plumbing.
Though I can enjoy hot water faucets,
deep wide sinks, grease-sucking drainpipes,

I don't want to live like that.
Having turned bowls up over bowls,
leaned plates against plates, laid
knives on a towel, I sponge the large bowl,
dump grime and bubbles in a bucket,
rinse, set upside-down on top the rack.
Then I wash the big pot and slide it
over the bowl so rims kiss, sides hug,

bottoms fit. As they drip, I lift
the waste water bucket, carry it outside
across the driveway. Crunchy snow,
lit stars, a three quarter moon
illuminating bushes and birch trees,
the below zero October air stings
fingers and throat. I grip the bucket bottom
and heave. Water cracks snow with a splash, steam

rising from the hole like a geyser.
Feet numb, hands clenched in sweater sleeves,
I follow vapor, watch the last wisp disappear
in moonlight, bright stars flickering.
Then I shut my eyes, wish, blow so hard I wince,
an icy stab to the chest. Opening my eyes,
my steaming cloud of breath forms a skull.
I hurry indoors, drop the bucket by the oven,

shake and rub my hands to thaw them.
Once they're warm I take my fiddle
and play one of those mournful, crooked,
West Virginia tunes. Sliding my fingers
up the neck, I stare at the dish rack,
the week's stack in perfect balance.
My 33rd birthday. It can't last.

Pipeline

Say scar on tundra
and I'll point north
to Prudhoe, tell you
to hike the jagged length
of pipeline to Valdez.

Begin mid-May, midnight,
the sun making coast
a blinding lunar desert
of bright ice, rotting snow,
pre-fab buildings, machinery—

a mirage of spring.
Follow the stitched land
south past slope, mountains,
an Interior of bugs.
Solstice, surveying

summer's daylong spill
on valley, imagine light
being pumped instead of oil.
Water and earth refined.
Straight to the terminus.

Big Moose Hits Truck

The wreckage: caved roof, exploded windshield,
blood, the body of a big cow moose
writhing on asphalt, a nearby calf bleating
like a goat. One witness, female, sought help.
The other, male, remained with the driver,
a mother who stood on the shoulder cradling
her two-year-old daughter. Both looked unhurt.
The mother shook telling the witness
how she swerved when the moose surged from brush.
Then it kept coming, aiming, smashed into her
as if on a date. She repeated the words—
on a date—and as she did looked strangely
beautiful, at peace. Then she shook harder,
hugged her child, told the witness her husband
had been killed last fall when he struck a moose.
At that moment the calf that had hovered
twenty yards away fled into the woods
shearing branches, leaves. Sunday morning,
the sun cut blue sky like a hatchet.

Two male troopers arrived. One shot the moose,
directed traffic. The other inspected
damage, asked what happened, wrote a report.
The witness who called the troopers returned
and took the mother and daughter home.
The other witness helped the troopers
sweep glass, push the truck off the road,
drag the big cow moose to the grass
where they butchered it. Near the end
they heard rustling, looked up, saw the calf
run across the road, spindly as a colt.
Without speaking, the three men went back
to slicing meat off the mother, a bright sun
splitting the late May day.

Past Milepost 135

Drowsing, I swerved and barely missed
a bear cub crossing the Parks Highway,
its wilder stretch between Talkeetna
and Cantwell. Four more hard hours
to Fairbanks, I veered onto the next
wide shoulder, slept, woke to a stranger
tapping the windshield, pointing
to a double rainbow arched over Denali.
I mumbled thanks, pushed myself up
out of the seat, stood, and watched
the sky pull color apart like taffy
while Denali, that big old mountain
of mountains, rose like the iceberg king,
shrugging sea level and humanity.
Breathing in the giant animal power
of this place, I settled once more
at the wheel, smelled the cool July air,
then spun onto blacktop, and took off
like a goshawk into the midnight pinks.

Learning Banjo

Right hand scrunched tight
into a claw, thumb out
like you need a lift,
knock the far first wire
with the right forefinger's nail,
and knock again, brushing
strings, your meaty stub
of a thumb following to pick
that short near high G.
Bum-titty, Bum-titty,
the tick-tocka, tick-tocka
of an old pocket watch
going loco. Pulling off
a fret with your left
ring finger, hammering on,
your blood like rye whiskey
bubbling in a still,
you sit yourself outside
on the front porch to twang
this strung long-necked drum
you'll one day frail fast
as fishtails in wild drunk time
for cross-tuned and wrecked
old-time Alaska fiddlers.

On the Tanana

This river trip, this passage,
we floated into a thick buzz
of mosquitos and no-see-ums,
the jams of snags, the trash
we thought had been recycled.
All week this tough country.

On a gravel landing then,
wind lucky, we dipped a net.
Three trout. One for you.
One for me. One to throw back
in exchange for a bugless,
safe, clean paddle to the end.

Fiddle Case

Crammed inside mine: rosin,
mute, eagle feather, two bows,
three-hundred-tune list,
spare strings, extra peg
and bridge, paper clips,
songbook, a few postcards,
band photos, music poems,
pens, banjo and guitar capos,
whiskey stain, a rough-looking
1910 instrument bartered for
in Chapel Hill, some coins—
including the mercury dimes
and mint buffalo nickel
a happy young woman tossed
as I buoyantly played
my heart out one twilight
on a ferryboat starboard
during that most wonderful
carefree sailing of my life.

Moonshine

The best ever was 4 a.m.
Sunday, Silver Falls
weekend, this blonde
mandolin player, too pretty
to be true, leaning way, way back
in her chair, playing dead
drunk. She was picking
a G tune, Ebenezer,
a hundred miles an hour—
right wrist floppy as a puppet's,
left fingers a flying
spider, lips and eyes
in that lovemaking grin beyond
knowing. Did she ever push
the fiddler on the high part.
Between tunes she pulled a pint
of corn whiskey from her case,
uncapped the jar, nipped,
and passed. Going down,
that shine burned wild
and bright as a rocket. God,
was it hot. Everything rang
when she kicked off the next.

Dance Hall, Fairbanks

God, you might say, how wild
and soft these creatures move.
Real sexy, as if early rut.
Yeah, tonight everyone's dancing

crackly tender—lovemaking
less the fuck, more like lust
earnestly opening its guts.
Men, jerky and strong. Women,
easy and tough. Inside,
no different. Rough spirits gliding.
The music making them fly.

Summer Snow, Fairbanks

A half foot fell, big flakes
quiet and strange as dandruff
parachuting like mad
out of summer's scalp.

I sat by the window
and scratched my own head:
the whole seeming world
had turned so suddenly

white a week before equinox.
As if to usher the winter
that would marry the darkness
that would conceive the wild

known as my Interior life.

Indian Summer at the Salvage Yard: a Flywheel Cover

He jumped off the forklift, pulled on goggles,
wiped a grimy hand on grimy coveralls.
I followed past doorless Fords,
rusted bumpers, tailpipes, pallets
of engines, transmissions, oily
scrap steel parts. Nothing's in place,
he said. Not a goddamned fucking thing.
I followed past gaping truck and schoolbus
bodies, the miscellaneous remains
hanging. We passed half an Army jeep,
THE PHANTOM someone had chalked
on glass. An orange sun shone
over rocks and weeds, over gravel,
over rows of Chevys—upholstery
ripped, windshields cracked,
headlights dangling like popped eyes.

What about this here, I pointed.
He slid under the front end
and I slid under too. I breathed in
the greasy metallic shade. Beneath that truck
he told me: The right one always comes up
and grabs you.

Miner's House, 9 a.m.

Passing through Delta, a stranger
in the only open cafe
for miles, I took a piss,
then a seat at the counter,
amused at the early hour
kerplunk of pool ball dropping
in pocket, men drinking
at the bar in the other room,
and ordered a cinnamon roll
without butter. Two hours
out of Fairbanks, November,
the land shelved in snow,
this slow redneck junction
had already long settled
into winter. Next minute,
served the big steaming bun,
a yellow scoop melting
in the goo, I let it go,
enjoyed the fat, like the sun
I saw that subarctic dawn
bleeding gold into Monday gray,
a distant unpolished metal
dissolving into light.

Christmas Eve at Alta's

—for Pete, his friends, and you

Here where winter is wintrier,
the way to stay sane is to make
each day from October to April
whole. That means attending
the stove, sitting for meals, feeding
the hound, and thanking the world
for this snug log home in the midst
of so much chill. Christmas Eve
blesses its simple good fortune.
Christmas arrives the moment
friends call, write, or visit.

II

Dance Camp

—for Tom Kizzia and Sally Kabisch

Maybe the perfect spot of land
is made of trees,
a floor of dusty dark planks
stomped on by dancers
as they balance and swing
to a New England fiddle
soaring over a syncopated
piano, the music a medley,
two reels and a hornpipe.

Or maybe the perfect spot of land
is someone to jitterbug with,
a partner who knows how
to hold hands, support
weight, look into eyes,
who knows why
you've got to keep time
to the music, that boogie-woogie
bass, a clear, clean sax.

Or maybe the perfect spot of land
is a honeymooning couple,
the first ones waltzing,
starting a snowball
within a solid ring
of best friends, the music
married to the sunlight
that shines past 11
in the Alaska spring.

Old-Time String-Band Jam

When three fiddlers sit
with a banjo player
and guitarist in chairs
tight in a closed
little ring, no matter
what you've been taught,
no matter your ear,
know when musicians bob
and sway and shake
like a flood of sound
dammed in a seat,
listen well. You'll hear
moonshine and mountain
joined at the peak,
a crooked creek crashing
its banks, a quick twist
of hindleg catching brush,
a leathery old rattler
slithering beneath.

John's Place

—*in memory of John Beckler*

May light made downtown Ester a gooey,
loose brown, made my rubber boots splash
and squish. The old post office lot,
the Golden Eagle lot, the Malemute lot:
all muck. Ten to ten, the forecast
called for overnight rain, high wind. Past
Cripple Creek Resort, John's beat-up Volvo,
parked at the fork, probably hadn't run
since October freeze-up. The first
dark clouds had swept over the dome

as I took the left and began walking
down the driveway, remembering last year's
late-night fiddle-banjo sessions
at King's Lake, Carlo Creek, Talkeetna—
the whiskey and beer, the music gossip,
Kate and Sally clogging on their boards.
I marched through a couple of gullies, sinking
deeper each step, and shook my head,
smiling. This impossible driveway
had gotten worse—even a jeep

had no chance now. Nobody ever came
to see him, John would complain, shrugging,
and then remember no one had time
to walk the mile-and-a-half in
without a guarantee. John had no phone—
no water or electricity either.
He'd squatted in the cabin for years,
then built a second room, a third,
then added a generator. He did
what he pleased. I first visited

four years ago, a gorgeous late May
morning, the birches all budding at once,
birds chirping everywhere, even from inside
the junked Volvo station wagon dead
on the left side of the driveway, halfway
in. Banging the banjo-shaped knocker
hanging from the door, I woke John.
But he didn't grouch letting me in,
and as he worked at the stove, I admired
the shelves and shelves of records

and tapes, the instrument boxes piled
in the far corner, the rough-looking piano
that John explained he had moved with help
of a dozen friends and Fairbanks-style
ingenuity. That morning we sipped mint tea,
ate toast with rhubarb jam, listened to Uncle Dave
Macon, to Dock Boggs, to the Red Clay Ramblers,
to the Horseflies and Chokers. John lent
a book of John Haines' poems. When I left
midafternoon we hugged, and I promised

to return. As I passed the Volvo wagon—now
all rust and mud—the first sharp drops hit.
The wind rose—birches swayed—the sky opened
and came down like an ax. I began jogging:
why hadn't I brought a flak jacket—
or a lousy six-pack—or my joke of a fiddle?
Why was I always getting soaked—
and arriving like a jerk? Why? Four years
it had taken—and I had nothing
for John. His book of poetry was still

on my shelf. I never thought. The rain
dumped harder then, and my blue workshirt
got plastered. Pounding through the slippery
crumbling slop, I made scant headway,
and leaned shivery into a blunt gusty
blast of squall. Jesus Christ—typical
Alaska weather. Five years in the state,
five winters, and here I was getting caught
unprepared. What was I doing living
up here? Sprinting up a slick little hill

I slid, almost fell, then tripped and sprawled
in a rut, a stupid tumble. Goddamnit—
I was a stinking muddy mess. John—
he'll probably think it's funny, my pants
brown and dripping. I picked myself up,
again started running, and flashed
to our first meeting—a rainy fall evening,
cool, the weather like tonight's, a party
off Goldstream. John, skinny, silvery-
black hair and moustache, looked unassuming

leaning against the corner, the outskirts
of the group. A cap propped on his head,
he was frailing his banjo, an A tune—
Wolves a Howling—and in the midst
John shut his eyes and started to howl,
a high, soulful whine that startled me,
gave me a chill I get when I'm touched.
John always sang like that. John—now
it was coming back: his place was just ahead.
Rain and wind, and now big hail chunks,

like bullets. Racing as best I could
in my rubber boots I dashed for the door.
John—I called twice, rapping my knuckles
against wood. John, I called. By my left foot
the banjo knocker lay sunk in the goo.
John, I called, pushing open the door.
Piano, instruments, shelves and shelves
of music: gone. Squirrels and mice had been
into things. But in John's place was a stove,
dry wood. I lit that fire in his name.

Burnt Down House

—for Jack Fontanella

The night of the cabin fire,
in the midst of cupboards
and kitchenware, closets
and clothes, when the flames
came picking, I like to think
how the two guitars, mandolin,
banjo, bass, and fiddle might have
jumped out of their skins
a moment to make the craziest
most raucous caterwauling noise,
enough riotous jabberwock
to fuel a dozen generations
of old-time string bands,
before slipping back into maple
to smoke hot and right,
the instruments' last bright
Denali festival of sound.

Karen's Place

I have something
for you, she said
and reached

into her pocket
and pulled
a map.

Back home
he took the map
to bed

and fell asleep
memorizing it
the light bulb on.

From the highway
a right turn
onto a half snow

half gravel road.
Past the one lane bridge
a left.

Down a mile
another right
then a left

then a right
each road snowier,
bumpier, climbing

then levelling,
the last road climbing
past an abandoned cabin

before narrowing,
a driveway,
tire tracks in snow

curving sharply,
a long rutted way
squeezed by trees.

From one tree
hung a tambourine;
from two others,

birdhouses;
from several,
yellow balloons

floated high
into the lit sky.
At the clearing

he parked his truck
next to hers.
Then he jumped out

and slammed the door.
Birds flew into bluish-white.
A rare wind gusted.

Everything shook and sang.
Inside the cabin
eyes waited like dice.

Up the hill
trees rose everywhere
and the ridge crested.

The In-Between Season

Like a black cat dyed bright blue and white,
the Alaska winter sky slyly hides
behind a blinding equinox sun
on snow, then a month-long April Fool's
slop known as break-up. In Fairbanks,
count on some genius in a new pickup
to take an unsafe Chena River ice road
shortcut, and get stuck, a good truck lost
to melting rot. In Anchorage, quick thinkers
speed on slippery hillside streets,
solve glaze and glare by sliding past stop signs
and skidding into Subarus with right-of-way.
And somewhere in the bush, guaranteed,
the arctic spring's mischievous freeze-and-thaw,
its miraculous eight minute per day climb
to light, will manufacture a long glassy fang
that will drip, drip, drip, drip,
and one frigid sunlit morning drop fifty feet
into the neck of an Eskimo kid—
death by icicle.

Caterpillars

When the moose that ravaged the carrots
      last summer reappears with calf,
when the first Canadian geese flap north
      as winged arrows over a field,
when the long light striking Murphy Dome
      throws shadows past eleven,
when the yard's lone aspen sapling buds,

when the woman wears to bed a shimmery
      violet diaphanous self,
when the man dreams of planting spinach
      in moist black soil,
when the last ancestral ghost exits
      to dissolve in air,
when the child sleeps through the night,

we will flutter to flowers as monarchs.

The Winter Years

Cold
oozed
pasty
through
the tube
of months,
squeezed
itself
empty
toward
spring,
that
long
dark
time
dying,
finally,
after
a last
snap,
a layer
of pre-
dawn
crackly
and thin
as skin
shed—

a grizzly
waking,
a lynx
sneaking,
geese
honking.

Fairbanks Cabin

My father, lifelong Philadelphian
visiting Alaska, could only see
I drove an old dented van and lived
in a small, mean, low-rent dwelling
with shabby plywood exterior, a peeling
front door that couldn't lock, drab
unmatched furniture, faded carpet,
a ladder leading up to God only knew.
A house without plumbing where I hauled
water from a spring ten miles away
and sat daily to contemplate digestion
in an outhouse with styrofoam seat.

Father, to have missed the arctic sky
that thrills; the utter privacy
and simplicity that comfort;
the blueberry bushes that feed;
the winter months that teach;
the heater that warms; the loft with desk,
typewriter, and mattress that realizes
my dreams. Father, that you traveled
five thousand miles and missed my being
saddens me. I only journey further.
What once had been is elsewhere.

Hitchhiking on Solstice, the Yukon

I begin at 8
and remain all day,
sun high, wind still,
mountains raw,
infrequent traffic
whistling past

as if I were invisible.
Perhaps I am
a caterpillar curled
in its cocoon,
or a night crawler
burrowed

from the dust.
In the 1 a.m. light,
as odd cars pass,
my thumb's shadow
eclipses my body.
I am arriving.

Fiddler

No time to practice new tunes,
he just listened to the same
four tapes on the car machine
a half hour each way
to and from work. At home,
bowed few minutes a week
so to fully attend family.

Fiddler, he took three seasons
to make them right tasty,
the thirty-nine new ones
that got planted in his ears,
became rooted in his head,
grew in him like peas. Fiddler,
all he had to do was be.

III

That Cramped and Stingy Sky

Begin with a little city
that on certain days smells
of the sea, its channel
like a tidal Mississippi.
Next, the steep mountains
that rise above downtown
each long winter as smug
white faces; and the others,
cross-channel, on an island
waiting to be scarred.
Despite the reports
that forecast more rain,
ice, darkness, and snow,
we know why developers
have chosen Juneau
for a new golf course,
a tram line, vacation
housing that won't dent
the city's 1% vacancy.
For this is southeast Alaska,
our next wild nowhere.

At Ebner Falls

The big gray stump like a totem
of an owl, October smell
of mud and leaf on a shoe,
I remembered the nightmare
about my grandfather—his face
a pale prune, his bony hands
and fingers tight to my neck—
and rose from the picnic bench,
touched the part of stump that jagged
like an ear, walked to the edge
of a rock. Staring up Gold Creek,
I might have caught a real owl
winging into the woods (though
I might have seen wind shaking
a branch, or my mind zippering open
like a suitcase). Everything roared
and something flew. Watching
froth shoot, I stepped back, turned
toward the falls, and let go
from the shoulder blades.
Then from the throat.

Front Street, Juneau

2 a.m., the sidewalk
in front of the Imperial Bar,
a snowy and blowing
November weekday night,
I could be in Nome:

Hero drunks murmuring
rocky truths to this
frostbit muse or that,
a murk thick as muscle
over an artificial frontier.

Tlingit from New Jersey

First month in Alaska,
the Indian punk escaped
his great-aunt, stole
a skiff, shot a deer
out of season, talked
extreme Bayonne trash
to a Sitka cop who tossed
his East Coast jive ass
in jail, parked him before
a desk, stuck a ballpoint
in his stubby left hand,
gave him forever.

Graveyard, Sitka

Past Observatory Street's dead end;
past the abandoned shed and broken glass;
past a recently fallen hemlock;
past sloshy trail, lush fern, old-growth spruce;
past the rusting truck bumper;
past a snarling feral cat;
past empty liquor bottles and beer cans;
past mud, rotting logs, mushrooms;
past the overgrown gravesites of Cyrus Williams, Jr. and Sr.;
past smells that might be fermented spirit;
past rain, rain, centuries of rain;
past plastic flowers, plastic wreaths, a plastic trash bag;
past John Sing (1896–1915), Agraphinna Hughes (1896–
1979),
      Mary Marks (1892–1992);
past the slippery downhill;
past two perched ravens cawing, an eagle flapping;
past link fence and pavement;
past the roar of a chain saw kicking in, another building
      going up.

Garbage Bears, Hoonah

I heard how one enterprising tour guide
drives summer visitors to the dump
to see local grizzlies paw mounds of trash
as they feed on rinds, peels, seeds, bones.
And how the high-schoolers approach
fearlessly in parents' pickups, honking horns,
lobbing beer cans, occasionally catching
a slow one from behind, front-bumper first.
Because I collect stories, I asked
to be taken, and was, the night after
the monsoon, gravel road mostly sloshy,
a full moon illuminating big smoke rising
from what must have been pit or ditch.
Three dark shapes nosed. Eyes flared,
quick incandescence amidst rubble.
They're eating America, I joked,
though no one laughed and it wasn't funny,
this view of large shadow creatures foraging
the land uphill from a small fishing town
accessible only by small plane or boat.
We sat silent then, until we too had our fill.

Fall Equinox, Hoonah

I stood on Hill Street's top step—
a spot I'd later learn
was known locally as Jackass Pass—
one extra second, watched a boat
motoring from the harbor. Nothing
for a moment, until I tilted
my face upward toward a big sun
that shone over the water, and stretched
my back. The word "I" disappeared
that instant, one beautiful
bright instant, before I reentered
myself, stretched once more, began
walking down the steps. Turning
toward the school, I saw a half moon
like a pale little cloud in sky.
And away from the school, beyond
the boat, a clearcut hill, almost fuzzy
in this wry and political
southeast Alaska light. Ah,
sun and moon—the usual argument.

Abstract of a Salmon Fisherman

For ten seasons I've trolled,
dark tails flapping
as I drag and raise the dying
heaviness. Exposed to the wet wind's

chill, I often question
the meaning of fishing.
My back and shoulders ache
even as I get paid. Arriving

home, I hug you and kiss your forehead.
You tell me salmon fishermen act
as naturally as salmon. I take your hands
and pretend we're swimming slowly

upstream to our creekbed. You catch me
by letting me be.

The Quilt
—for Halli Kenoyer

Square after crazy square
she sews sixty-four wild
bright Ketchikan snatches:
a banjo, a fiddle, a clogger
buckdancing, a couple balance-
and-swinging, lovers waltzing,
a mother nursing, a father
seining, boats bobbing, salmon
spawning, a dock, a seesaw,
a tall spruce falling,
a woodstove firing, clouds,
rain on water, rain on mountains,
rain splattering roofs, rain
like a fist, rain like kisses,
rain hissing like a snake,
mist, drizzle, downpour, leak,
rain on a tent, rain in a face,
slush, bog, skunk cabbage, ducks
on a lake, ravens on a wire,
swallows on a feeder, a dog
on a bed, an old weathered house,
a row of tulips, yellow roses,
swollen berries, a rippling creek,
a winding street, big bookshelves,
a quick joke, a trick knot,
a magical snicker, chocolate cake,
ice cream pie and cookies, sweet
bite-sized children, a girl fingering
a lunchbox, a girl saddling
a pony, a girl tickling
the moon, a girl circling
the sun, an all-girl world,
a boy for every girl,
a man for every woman,
a song for every family,
a psalm for every island,

spirit grinding like a mill,
a heart spiraling with stars,
spilt ghosts, stilted beams,
a partner and a trail,
a wholly blue sky,
a smile wicked with teeth,
a spring eager for heat,
a summer threaded to light.

Jon Sherman's Farewell from Juneau

For this mandolin-picking buddy's departure
from the slop, swash, and fellowship
of southeast Alaska, I sat at the piano,
composed a bouncy New England dance melody
I hoped caught the flavor of this gentle
red-haired man's freckles and grin, his oddly
right sense of time, his rhythmic drive,
then fiddled it as he boarded the ferry south.

Since that May evening, he's moved to Durango,
Wellfleet, some small town up the Maine coast,
and now, I'm sure, to yet one more spot
near mountain or ocean, far from crowds,
close to the natural tuning of his heart,
this latest place so crackling with passion
an electric sky will power his music onward:
the next inevitable cross-country flight.

IV

Cacophonous Country

The plump will gripe. Saps,
all of them. Flatulent
phlegmatic plutocrats. Cinch
and spit. Brassy asses.
Politics to the nth. Churchy
kitsch. Cupidity's match.
Crunchy roast beef pilgrims.
Jazzed treacheries. A mundane
unassuming sitcom. Somebody,
Help! Bloody godly assumptions.
True as the classifieds,
musical as a cog or crutch,
these noisy Americans.

Mr. X, Mr. Y, Mr. Z

Aging white men, the Alaskans
of Washington D.C. carry
the worst traits of my father
times three. Cranky old-timer,
slicko charmer, greedy dealmaker,
he saw the world as toy oyster:
I have mine—so if you don't
have yours, boy, you must not be open
to the opportunities. Ah yes,
opportunities. My dad, dogged
salesman, made a small fortune
peddling printing from Raleigh
to Boston, ruining his family
in the process. He was barely home.
Alaska's far servants, Mr. X,
Mr. Y, Mr. Z—I know them
as I knew my father: a crotchety
and condescending East Coast geezer,
thousands of miles out of touch.

Three Alaskans

One Alaskan legislator
confused *indigent*
with *indigenous,*
then joked the words
identical. And laughed.

One Alaskan legislator
(this one serving in D.C.)
came home to tell high-schoolers
that funding art was wrong:
"Some artists celebrated buttfucking."

And one indigent heterosexual
white male writer, me,
would never ever say *buttfucking*
to high-schoolers, indigenous
or not. Except in this poem.

We Are All One

At the party that night
I told a poet friend:
By aiming my venom
at our congressman
and senators—at least
I'd hit the culprits.

But wait, he said,
we're their kin
and more—the world's
a family of cells
spinning as bodies
in God's spring wind.

Then we suffer stomach
and lung cancer,
I said, eyes on
my friend's belly,
then throat, then eyes
that avoided mine.

A Nation that Grows, Grows, Grows

An atmosphere out of kilter,
where the seasons turn
warm, warmer, warm, will grow
dams, dust, nursery schools
as the fields and creeks diet
on chemical and drought.

Politicians without controls
who gather and hoard as squirrels
will grow tall bankrolls
and climb, clawing upward,
to trade tax dollars
for a special status quo.

Governments without souls
where the line is grow
will clearcut older trees,
manufacture more weapons
and charge it to development,
research, security, youth.

Industries without centers
whose faces are drawn
by blank little men, grow big
on microchips, transistors,
cigarettes, pharmaceuticals,
TV, six-packs of watery beer.

I Dreamed I Was in His Republican Brain

Don't blame me, I didn't ask
for this vision: gray and coiled
clouds, smoke, sparkly synapses
misfiring, me in a hardhat
struggling through the fog.
What groans. Pain, like a jawbone
snapping. Pointing my headlamp
downward, I catch a far soul
fighting shameful memories. What,
I can't tell. A thicket or jungle.
A houseful of beasts squawking.
Something's missing. I grapple
to learn, but can't. Waking,
I view the words: *A poor man—*
damaged and inaccessible.

I Dreamed I Was in His Republican Heart

I descend, slipping through the dark
chambers, soft walls beating caco-
phony, then collapsing in purplish
swirl. Ornery smells. Barn-
yard rubble. God help, I moan.
Sound muffled by a bloody swell
of muscle and pump. Sad blanket,
I think, and feel my skin shrink
from cold muddled Yukon sludge.
Trapped, I fear. Then watch amazed
as the thick gooey ooze turns
into a black-and-white contract to hate.

See the Senator, Hear the Senator, Speak the Senator

I see the Senator
in every stiff neck, every crooked crack,
every chronic backache and skin rash,
every lucky snake's ready slither.

I hear the Senator
in every loud quip, every empty objection,
every officious political trick,
every cash drawer's rude knock.

I speak the Senator
when I smell crude oil and scorn,
when I mistake forest for pulp,
when I point to big industry's pawn.

One Halloween Party I Wore a Republican Mask

Heh heh heh, friends, I'll let you in
on a secret, I don't own Alaska,
just borrowing it from the creatures here.
Caribou, bear, moose, wolf, sheep—shit,
what isn't there to hunt and eat. Yes,
like I was saying, friends, eat up, eat up.
Oh, isn't that a twist. Look at that. The Senator
from North Carolina has spray-painted himself
green, for godsakes. Heh heh heh, you rebel
rascal. Who'd have guessed. Oh, sorry,
you're what? Paperless money? Okay, right
buddy. Whatever you say. Well now,
over there by the lamp, now that's original.
Our Speaker of the House with a crowd around him,
thousand-dollar bills taped to his books.
(Hmmm, next year I can come as his shadow
if I can find a wig plastered just right.)
Folks, drink up. And congressmen, senators,
to clean and sharpen the teeth, your very own
initialed Tongass National Forest toothpicks.
Heh heh heh, heh heh heh, cut just last week.

PA SMY

—for Dee

Not the name of an irritable
Carolina tobacco farmer,
or a coot of a butcher
with a thumb on the scale,
or a thick-armed good ol' boy
gas station/mini-mart owner,
but the inverse. Think
commonsense Alaskan, the son,
grandson, and great-grandson
of commonsense Vermonters,
a plain man who reads the news
that ANWR (the Arctic National
Wildlife Refuge) is now AOR
(the Arctic Oil Reserve),
and finds himself suddenly jerked
into alert. "Don't know what
they're up to, but can't be good,
changing names like that," says
PA SMY (People Against Small-
Minded Yahoos). "VOTE THEM OUT
(Vain Old Thickwitted Egocentric
Tightwads—Hell, Earth Makes
Our Universe Tick). Hell yes,
we've got to vote them out
before the bastards destroy
what all we've got left."

Certain Lawmakers, Lawyers, Lobbyists, Aides

Ethics shmethics, reform or no reform,
we can still launder this, lay off that,
learn to leak a little here, a little there,
deal with the lousy lefties when we have to.
Next, with their logic, the liberals will say
we can't legislate. Fuck 'em, the liars.
Let's hit 'em with suits, shut some rec centers
and libraries. Sure, they'll spit and sputter—
until they back down and beg they need us
once we point to some loophole or other.
The saps get off when we pinch their asses,
whisper something sweet, then come like hammers.
Gentlemen, we'll discuss details over lunch.

Glenn

My best and worst composition student
that year, Glenn used to hang after class
to spout beliefs that invariably led to
"Sir, morally I view you stepping off
a curb, and into the path of a truck—
don't you see it's my duty to save you."
Glenn oozed a glibness so righteous and facile—
facile, the exact word for his gift.
Adopted by missionaries, raised Christian,
at the time an assured and ambitious
Young Republican, Glenn wrote easily
as breath. Early work earned effortless "A's,"
though the ten-page research paper that compared
the world's religions so as "to prove"
his own church superior forced me to repeat
what I preached in conference: for this class,
the approach for this topic would be
to first assess *the difficulty* in comparing
every religion, which was a worthy paper alone,
and then to write *an objective analysis*
of *every* religion, which would take many pages,
and then, and only then, he could get on
with his theory, which, while *very* risky,
he was free to try. So, when I told him
that because he didn't follow directions
(he had lumped Buddhism, Hinduism, Judaism,
and the rest in a single paragraph, had never
mentioned, much less solved, the dilemma of scope),
and used only tracts from his church's
publishing house, plus the Bible, as sources,
and thus he would fail unless he revised,
Glenn flashed a murderous glance, sulked a week,
and the next Friday delivered a heartless
"A" paper on capital punishment in Alaska.
Later, learning his grade, he beamed:
"Sir, someday I'll run for political office—
that way I can save you and everybody.
What do you think?" I remain vigilant.

Suffering Democracy

Instead of a gun, or knife,
or pill, or drink. Or punching
the wall, the dog, screaming
at kids. Or holding
too many pains too deep—
brutal parents, cruel lovers,
bad bosses, debts, illnesses,
dying friends, extinct creatures,
absent God, near-ruined planet.

First, grip a pen, and write.
Then, pick a place, and plant.
Then, be patient, and let grow.
Then, enter a small booth,
pull around the blue curtain,
kiss that ballot, and vote.

V

Nome before Man

Cross a bridge
into the wind,
fog, and dark.

Hunt stars.
Trap sunlight,
heat, farawayness.

Harness speed,
grip tight,
and fly

for the moon,
but slip on ice,
and drop, spilling

the green fire
that ushers
midnight.

Reincarnate
as gold nuggets,
dust, beach,

a heavy winter
on the edge
of earth.

Iliapuq

My single vocabulary word
of Siberian Yup'ik I learned
from Vince Okpealuk, a wiry
chain-smoking Inupiat Eskimo
from Wales, a self-described
whaler, carver, reindeer herder,
carpenter, guitarist, book reader,
ornery and loving father of six.
My former top student, Vince
had spent a season in Viet Nam,
bummed San Francisco's Haight
on acid in the mid-sixties,
journeyed home to marry,
then lost himself in the drunk
that is Nome's Front Street,
a fellowship of bars that grip
with a quick alcoholic squeeze.
Buzzed St. Lawrence Islanders
taught Vince to say *iliapuq*,
meaning, literally, orphan,
or, in that dialect's slang,
one who finds parents in a bottle.

The Gluepot

Off-balanced, having tripped over the moon,
I stumbled up and down Front Street,
fell into the Anchor, that old Nome haunt
like a curse, every face lost in the same
lifelong search for a god that had gotten drunk,
straddled the land, fucked her, passed out,
then skipped town, another deadbeat father.

I left my companions to brood in that choice
narrow bar, and crossed toward the Gluepot,
the only cafe open late. Mid-August,
still dusk, wind from some darker place
cut like a band saw. Stepping past
a staggerer, I ducked inside to order
the extra-large bowl of reindeer stew,

and was greeted in that slow familiar
village-English, a cadence basic and square
as a hut. I looked, caught young Natives
crowding around pinball and video games,
older Eskimos sitting at the front tables,
eating hamburgers, conversing softly.
The only white person in the room, I turned,

and heard that voice again: *You've come,
I didn't think I would see you again.*
It's you, I said, spotting him, my ghost
brother grinning at the counter, a phantom
with teeth. I took the stool beside him,
and ate my fill in silence, a spirit
shimmering with the music of grace.

Parsonage

No home, for three weeks
my unrolled sleeping bag
graced the living room
of the Methodist church's
parsonage. In that sanctuary,
masturbating twice nightly
(my climactic fantasies
focused on a devout Christian
woman with a terrific body),
my slow, dark fiddling
won the devil's regard.

Though I was guilty
that first Nome month of lying
on the carpet and lusting
for another man's wife,
I slept secure, deep
in the dreamless sleep
of the churchgoing righteous.
My sin was nothing
that would keep me from heaven:
I had the clergyman's faith
in the divine, forgiving future.

Inside a Unalakleet House

Last night you dreamed
that as your parents
slept, you rose ghost-like
from bed, opened a window,
flew. Warm for October,
a half moon blocked by clouds,
you soared toward King Mountain,
two hundred miles northwest.

Your father's 86. Your mother's 83.
What will become of them?
And you, the youngest,
the only one not to leave
the village. What of you?

As you were about to climb,
the haze broke. Below,
the knobbed top of King Mountain.
Midnight, you almost believed
faint light still shone
far northwest. But no.
On that dark summit you turned,
faced the Big Dipper,
and knelt.

End of February, Unalakleet

The way you said it: the sting
that claws your face. And I'm taken
to other Februaries, other places,
the roar of snowmachiners on their way
to the gym, leaving the gym,
heading upriver, returning.
Other Januaries too. And Decembers.
Bitter blizzard-making wind.
Windless days too, sometimes.
How often I've smelled the stink
of exhaust, then next minute
heard only the silence of ice
and sky. That's Unalakleet,
yet one more coast village
busy clawing back at winter.

Teller Road

Beyond the last cabin, past the Cape Woolley turn-off,
everywhere a raging yellow and orange celebration
beneath clear October sky, and each time I decided

to park the truck, stride solo miles to enjoy this
triumphant autumn wilderness afternoon, a voice inside
commanded: Drive on. So, past one long stretch

with a view of a most spectacular empty desolation,
and past another with curve after curve of tundra
consumed in its fire, I finally pulled off

at the exact highest point of road, grabbed sweaters
and pack, slammed the door, then began hiking
toward the tallest near peak. Atop that summit

I sat crosslegged watching the sharp sun inflame this
little-known land, making the most beautiful spot
on earth for a moment, the most beautiful spot ever.

And already, that quickly, the far hills were in shade.
Despite layers, I was shivering. Rising, I knocked dirt
off my pants. If I hurried downhill and drove,

I could catch one more prime Nome sunset.
Ah, but what kind of world demands yet one more
big bright ball falling into horizon,

one more streaked red-and-pink sky darkening
in pursuit? Asking that question, and others,
I dawdled back to town in the cool.

Nome Preacher

Unlike his simple missionary brethren
who considered Nome a tolerable
if savage place, the Baptist preacher
felt *it* in his gut, and finding *it*
everywhere, wrote *it* Thursday mornings
in bed, revised *it* Friday afternoons
at his desk, rehearsed *it* all Saturday,
delivered *it* twice Sundays in church.

The congregation quickly awakened
to that presence by organizing
committees, meeting in living rooms,
contacting higher-ups, threatening
to run that devil preacher fellow
clear to Kansas. He responded
first with prayer, then Prozac.
His tenth month, he left for Texas.

This Valentine's Day, I Write You from Eek

So happy this winter day shines
over a village near the mouth
of the Kuskokwim. So happy,
the sun rising so high now over ice,
a world so shiny and new
this February, like always. So happy
that Juneau and the politics
are so far away, this state legislature
so cruel I think of my father,
a 230 pound man who bullied
little kids. Perhaps the capital
should move to Eek, so lawmakers
might experience the mysteries
of love, nature, spirit,
and understand there are greater forces
than themselves. But I know
even then they will not learn
until the day they suffer enough,
or their children suffer enough,
or their grandchildren suffer enough
from the effects of ill-conceived
tort reform, poorly funded schools,
mismanaged private prisons, dirty air,
dirty water, someone else's pain
caused by their own skewed logic.
And, yes, someday they will suffer.
For in Eek I am happy to report
a scoured universe, its perfect
and particular justice a long cold view
of darkness. And light.

A Week in Eek

Kids in sneakers squeaking across
the Eek School gym floor, streaking towards
baskets. Or else sneaking out of class
to steal a smoke, or a peek at an uncle's
or cousin's sleek new Arctic Cat. Meek kids.
Cheeky kids. Rural-chic kids. Geeks.
Kids that speak weakened Yup'ik
and village English that leaks articles,
the and *a* in particular, making
language go creak so nice. Eek winter days—
not quick, not slow, just a dark freaky trick
like the snaky bow of a rogue bachelor *gussuk*
playing fiddle those decades back. Unique Eek.
Where weeks pass in a day. An hour lasts weeks.
Times as wild as any Dr. Seuss might seek.

43rd Birthday, Eek

Y-K Delta creeks on the cusp of slushy,
clouds on truce for a day, I flew
once more to that village near the mouth
of the Kuskokwim. Eye, it means
in Yup'ik, though no one could say
if eye referred to those few good yards
of elevation in a vast white flatlands
or its spot amidst water. Eek, I say,
in English. Eek, like a mouse or small bird.
Eek, like an echo. Eek, like screechy fiddle.
Eek, like a high school kid with pencil vexed
at the intricacies of language. Eek, Eek,
like a sixth grader in sleeping bag jabbering
to a pal after lights out. Eek, Eek, the reply.
Eek, Eek, fireworks sizzling. Or fizzling.
Eek, Eek, Eek, my third consecutive year.
A celebration of ice cream and cake, candles,
many young friends whose names I'll never know.

Eek Authors' Festival, Year Four

Visiting Eek, brave *gussuks* like me joke
we'll hitch back to Bethel on snowmachine
in forty-below chill. Bouncing between
cultures, sharp *gussuks* like me note diet coke
and computer, caribou and dear folk
who don't bounce, but ride naturally between
Yup'ik and English, tundra and TV. I've been
to Eek four times now, fiddling *gussuk* who'll poke
around later with pen, finding something
to write. Sweet Eek, I'll scribble, recalling
cold morning showers in the school, a good sleep
in sleeping bag on library floor, the deep peep
of Eek kids. And from Quinhagak and Kasigluk,
shy whisperers, homesick despite friends and books.

The Lights of Nightmute

A late January night, Toksook Bay,
I caught six hundred stars,
what slivery moon the frozen
tide brought. Twenty miles across
the ice, the lights of Nightmute,
like dozens and dozens of fallen stars.
That old village shone. Close enough
to squint into the future, see
an April plane crash that would kill
two, then glimpse the Juneau body
of mostly railbelt Republicans
with no love for Native history or brains
debate the bill that would cut
education in the Bush as easily
as overhunt moose, overfish salmon,
make one more thoughtless, racist crack.

A late January night, Toksook Bay,
I felt the lights of Nightmute shiver
with the insight that technology
has overtaken us, so the lights
of Bethel are now not so far away,
the lights of Anchorage now not so far away,
the lights of Juneau now not so far away—
Juneau's arrogant and greedy twinklings
a stupid dim power from down near Seattle.

A late January night, Toksook Bay,
I heard a line of snowmachines roar
through the village like the beginning
or end of a race, as if to remind me
there are still far places to go,
wonderfully crucial ways to live
that the smug white lawmakers
working out of Juneau will never know.
For them, I offer one more
rainy foggy southeast morning,
the better to look inside and listen
to their own folk music—
a slick, self-righteous fiddling.

This Day, Barrow

Almost noon, moon over tundra,
light shining on sea ice, I say
beautiful to myself, aware that if
I were to write it, one ex-professor
would say: Explain it—what gives you
the right? And the chorus of editors
would complain: nothing original or new.

Ah, but it *is* beautiful, I repeat
as I watch the tip of dawn sway
the dark, another night being peeled
layer by layer. *Beautiful, beautiful,*
I think, going back to my business,
which is to seek out far horizons,
then record their favorite word.

Ah, Barrow

Conceive a port north
past the Books Range.
Let the seven April shades
of white—fog, blizzard,
ice, horizon, cloud,
wide windswept tundra, sun—
determine spring. Subtle,
but not. Foreign, but not.
The light encompasses, yes?
Squint into the totality, this
wryly bright picture. Then
say to yourself, yes,
you've come to the old orphan
love-child of heaven and moon—
the frozen way-station home.

Cinco de Mayo, Barrow

The first week of whaling, windchill
minus fifteen despite a twenty-three-hour
sun, the Mexicans of Barrow gather at Pepe's,
the world's most northern taco and burrito
eatery. Having survived yesterday's big snow,
some celebrate by blankly looking out
at the taxis disappearing in the latest
ground blizzard to swirl up off the streets.
One or two, their sense of cinema intact, think:
Bunuel. The rest have long shut their eyes
and ears to the Inupiat Eskimos who own the town,
the Filipinos and whites more newly arrived,
the nine-month winter all residents suffer,
and focus on the knife, the fork, the plate
in front of them. Replaying today's work
(calculating wage yet again), the hungriest
believe if they're only hungry enough,
they'll taste, taste, taste their way home.

Top of the World

—for Dave Putnam

The finest old-time fiddler
north of the Arctic Circle
taught me a half dozen tunes
I'd immediately forgotten
but my fingers might recall
if I could revisit the vast
Barrow midwinter spring
of early May. Past whalers
camped near sea ice ready
to crack, I'd again accompany
that fiddler on an easy dig
into the further histories
of our musical race, until
we came to the slow twisty
crookedness elusive and plain
as the first tiny needles
on this or that young pine
bent and struggling for light
up a West Virginia peak.
There we'd sit, knowing
even as we turned over
that site again and again
everything to the south
was busy in bud, playing
something modal beneath.

VI

To Live on this Earth

                If you can forgive
our feet,
        that used-up clay;
our legs,
        those stilted roots;
our hips,
        that late May frost;
our crotch,
        that dredged gold;

                if you can forgive
our spine,
        that lost pole;
our belly,
        those oily waters;
our ribs,
        those stricken elms;
our heart,
        that dark granite;

                if you can forgive
our arms,
        that miscarried bomb;
our hands,
        those shaken victims;
our fingernails,
        that clickety quiet;
our touch,
        that toxic snap;

       if you can forgive
our tongue,
     that windblown trash;
our eyes,
     those shrouded suns;
our brow,
     that nonstop factory;
our hair,
     that wasted acre;

       if you can forgive
our blood,
     that spoiled mush;
our bones,
     those spent shells;
our sickness,
     that ready looter;
our selves,
     those fateful birthrights—

we can bear anything, Mother.

September 11, 2001

This is no poem
about planes hijacked and flown
into New York City buildings,
cameras catching the surreal, endless
snippets—some edited, some not—
of towers on fire awhile,
then suddenly collapsing, the heap
a mix of concrete, dark
smoke, bodies, ash, everywhere
the rubble—and that ignores
a third plane hijacked and flown
into the Pentagon, a fourth
plowing into a Pennsylvania field,
the thousands dead. That's the poem
television writes. Underneath is another—
strange world of good and evil,
love and hate, great anger
and even greater faith.
Nothing ever changes. Everything has.
We'll need friends, family, music.
A language that transcends.

At the Survival General Store

We begin each day with two dollars
and a choice: a loaf of bread,
or a map. And always we've chosen
a round wedge of warm sourdough
with thick crust, and enjoyed it
hunk by hunk, wandering the earth
under lit gray skies through which
we could almost see tomorrow.

Yesterday, hemmed by rock and ice,
we chose map for the first time,
and learned we were in Survival,
a semi-depressed mineral town
halfway between Payne and Salvation.
Accordingly, we swiped a loaf,
ran for the cutoff, and entered
the trailhead that led to the pass.

To Feed on Seed, or Star

Everything so wet and warm,
the world all rain and roots,
an earth neither destroyed
nor renewed, fog sewed the day
in a quilt of windstorm
and reverence, and so I watched
the hound push forward, snout
to path, sniffing fungus
and leaves like some gargantuan
four-legged hairy worm
creeping through the dirty
autumn green. Tail pointing,
the canine trembled a moment,
then suddenly pawed a mound
that must have been home
to families of crawling things,
digging as if for a bone,
which for you or me might mean
seed, or star, or dream.

The Way They Eat
—for Paul and Deb

Summer, they manage ingeniously,
the near-daily grocery run from a far
Fairbanks cabin, their Murphy Dome clearing
home to cookstove, root cellar, beer cooler,
long-lit evenings of neighbors, cohorts,
experimentally spiced delicacies.

Winter, they survive the village:
first hunting, fishing, gathering
what that peninsula wilderness provides;
then foraging the edibles flown in from Nome.
Two foreigners passing through, night
after night a seemingly endless stew.

In between, invariably the dream
of some exotic but familiar kitchen
stocked with what is local and true. There,
dirty dishes in the sink subject to debate,
appliances hum with contentment and grace:
an artist-husband, his writer-wife.

A + B = Miracle

Everything is broken, or dies:
a window, a season, a fish.
So, first there is damage.

Add to it the sunrise, an earth
that encompasses the grace
of calendars, the laying on
of hands, the prophets and mystics,
Christmas and New Year's, madrigals
and canticles, the work of birth.
Go back in time then, and undo.
That is what equals miracle.

Mother Parabola

—for Karen

How this earth moves
in its plainly strange way,
allowing us paper, pen,
the bent to laugh and jest
with language, then to
get serious, use short serious
words like *cancer,* big serious
words like *contraception.*
Fortunate pilgrims. We have
stock to slaughter, desert
to wander, oasis to sate,
straight line to harp on,
long slow curve to live.

William Stafford atop Mt. Ripinski

Forty-two hundred feet closer
to an August sky the clear blue
of eyes, having climbed a last breezy
bare-rock mound beyond meadow and bush,
he faced up to heaven and saw
past his desire to love and be loved,

until he sat to take in that rare
long view of southeast Alaska water
and wood. Rapt, he dug in his pack
for an apple, cheese, a book
which he read from. Then he slept,
his head on worn paper cover,
through which spoke the poems.